This book belongs to

_Irene Bergen_

# Bless All Who Serve

*Sources of Hope, Courage and
Faith for Military Personnel
and Their Families*

Matthew and Gail Tittle, Editors

Skinner House Books
Unitarian Universalist Association of Congregations
Boston

Copyright © 2010 by the Unitarian Universalist Association of Congregations. All rights reserved. Published by Skinner House Books, an imprint of the Unitarian Universalist Association of Congregations, a liberal religious organization with more than 1,000 congregations in the U.S. and Canada.

Unitarian Universalist Association of Congregations
Peter Morales, President
25 Beacon St.
Boston, MA 02108-2800

Printed in the United States

Cover and text design by Jeff Miller

ISBN 1-55896-566-1
978-1-55896-566-9

6 5 4 3 2 1
12 11 10

Bless all who serve : sources of hope, courage, and faith for military personnel and their families / Matthew and Gail Tittle, eds.
        p. cm.
    ISBN-13: 978-1-55896-566-9 (pbk. : alk. paper)
    ISBN-10: 1-55896-566-1 (pbk. : alk. paper)    1. Soldiers—Prayers and devotions.    2. Unitarian Universalist Association—Prayers and devotions.    I. Tittle, Matthew.    II. Tittle, Gail.
    BX9855.B64 2010
    242'.88—dc22

                                                            2010003864

Note: Skinner House Books and the Unitarian Universalist Association of Congregations are committed to the use of gender-inclusive language. For the sake of accuracy, however, quoted material has been printed as originally written.

Copyright acknowledgments are on pages 93–106 and on the final page.

# Contents

Dear Reader,

Whether you are a soldier, a sailor, an airman, or marine, or simply someone who loves and supports a member of the military, we offer you this small collection of readings in recognition of your service. As we selected each piece for this volume, we asked ourselves, "Will this be meaningful to those serving today, whether in non-combat situations or in harm's way?" You will find here a wide variety of selections from many faith traditions and religious perspectives that will comfort, challenge, and inspire. Whether in the field or front lines, at sea or on base, at home or in the chapel, *Bless All Who Serve* is meant to be just that—a blessing to all soldiers, sailors, airmen, and marines—past, present, and future—and their families.

We are deeply honored to be the editors of *Bless All Who Serve*. We wish such a resource had been available during our own years of military service. Gail served as an active duty Air Force officer for fourteen years, achieving the rank of major. Before becoming a Unitarian Universalist minister, Matthew served as an active duty naval officer for eleven years and as a reservist for another nine years, retiring as a commander.

This volume is possible only through the generous contributions of many donors who wanted to affirm the work of military personnel and chaplains around the world. We would like to thank the Unitarian Universalist Association president, Rev. Peter Morales, for his support of this project. A dedicated group of military chaplains contributed their passion and insight to shaping the book. And last but not least, we would like to express our gratitude to Rev. Cynthia Kane and Rev. Lisa Presley, whose advocacy was instrumental in making this book a reality.

In all that we do, may love be our guide, may passion be our strength, and may courage be our way.

Matthew and Gail Tittle
*Houston, Texas*

# Ancient Texts

Finally, beloved,
whatever is true,
whatever is honorable,
whatever is just,
whatever is pure,
whatever is pleasing,
whatever is commendable,
if there is any excellence
and if there is anything worthy of praise,
think about these things.

—PHILIPPIANS 4:8


Blessed are the poor in spirit,
    for theirs is the kingdom of heaven.
Blessed are those who mourn,
    for they will be comforted.
Blessed are the meek,
    for they will inherit the earth.

Blessed are those who hunger and thirst for
    righteousness,
  for they will be filled.
Blessed are the merciful,
  for they will receive mercy.
Blessed are the pure in heart,
  for they will see God.
Blessed are the peacemakers,
  for they will be called children of God.
Blessed are those who are persecuted for
    righteousness' sake,
  for theirs is the kingdom of heaven.
Blessed are you when people revile you and
    persecute you
  and utter all kinds of evil against you falsely
    on my account.
Rejoice and be glad, for your reward is great in
    heaven,
  for in the same way they persecuted the
    prophets who were before you.

—MATTHEW 5:3–12

Our Father in heaven,
hallowed be your name.
Your kingdom come,
Your will be done
on earth, as it is in heaven.
Give us this day our daily bread.
And forgive us our debts,
as we also have forgiven our debtors.
And do not bring us to the time of trial,
but rescue us from evil.

—MATTHEW 6:9–13


In days to come
the mountains of the Lord's house
shall be established as the highest of the mountains,
and shall be raised above the hills;
all the nations shall stream to it.

Many peoples shall come and say,
"Come, let us go up to the mountain of the Lord,
to the house of the God of Jacob;
that he may teach us his ways
and that we may walk in his paths."

For out of Zion shall go forth instruction,
And the word of the Lord from Jerusalem.

He shall judge between the nations,
and shall arbitrate for many peoples;
they shall beat their swords into plowshares,
and their spears into pruning hooks;
nation shall not lift up sword against nation,
neither shall they learn war any more.

—Isaiah 2:2–4


The Lord is my shepherd, I shall not want.
He makes me lie down in green pastures;
he leads me beside still waters;
he restores my soul.
He leads me in right paths for his name's sake.

Even though I walk through the darkest valley,
I fear no evil;
for you are with me.
your rod and your staff—they comfort me.

You prepare a table before me in the presence of
  my enemies;

you anoint my head with oil;
my cup overflows.
Surely goodness and mercy shall follow me all the
    days of my life,
and I shall dwell in the house of the Lord
my whole life long.

—Psalm 23


Where can I go from your spirit?
Or where can I flee from your presence?
If I ascend to heaven, you are there;
If I make my bed in Sheol, you are there.
If I take the wings of the morning
and settle at the farthest limits of the sea,
even there your hand shall lead me,
and your right hand shall hold me fast.
If I say, "Surely the darkness shall cover me,
and the light around me become night,"
even the darkness is not dark to you;
the night is as bright as the day,
for the darkness is as light to you.

—Psalm 139:7–12

For everything there is a season,
and a time for every matter under heaven:
a time to be born, and a time to die;
a time to plant, and a time to pluck up what is
    planted;
a time to kill, and a time to heal;
a time to break down, and a time to build up;
a time to weep, and a time to laugh;
a time to mourn, and a time to dance;
a time to throw away stones, and a time to gather
    stones together;
a time to embrace, and a time to refrain from
    embracing;
a time to seek, and a time to lose;
a time to keep, and a time to throw away;
a time to tear, and a time to sew;
a time to keep silence, and a time to speak;
a time to love, and a time to hate;
a time for war, and a time for peace.

—ECCLESIASTES 3:1–8

The finest weapons are the worst evils. They are universally loathed. Therefore, help guide your nation to the non-aggressive path.

The wise hold steady on the passive yin path. Those who are aggressive prefer the active yang.

Weapons are instruments of coercion and devils of death. Resort to them only in dire necessity. Peace is our natural state of being.

If weapons must be wielded to defend ourselves, and we are victorious, never rejoice. Can there be joy over the slaughter of others?

On joyous occasions we attune with the yang side. On sad occasions, with the yin.

During battle, the soldiers are on the left yang side, engaging in combat. The commanders are on the right yin side, observing the action.

After the battle, the soldiers who have slain others, move to the yin side and mourn. While the commanders, now on the yang side, are celebrating victory even though it is a funeral.

—TAO TE CHING, 31

The best soldier fights without vengeance, without anger and without hate.

He puts himself humbly below his comrades, thereby eliciting the highest loyalty from them.

This is the power of non-belligerence and cooperation. It is the ancient path to the Great Integrity.

—TAO TE CHING, 68

They that are desirous of victory do not conquer by might and energy so much as by truth, compassion, righteousness, and spiritual discipline. Discriminating then between righteousness and unrighteousness, and understanding what is meant by covetousness, when there is recourse to exertion, fight without arrogance, for victory is there where righteousness is. Under these conditions know, O king, that to us victory is certain in this battle. Indeed, where Krishna is, there is victory.

—MAHABHARATA, BHISHMA PARVA 21

A blessing is contentment for whatever there be,
A blessing is the wholesome deed at the end of life,
A blessing it is to relinquish all sorrow.

A blessing in the world is reverence for mother,
A blessing, too, is reverence for father,
A blessing in the world is reverence for the recluse,
A blessing, too, is reverence for the scripture.

A blessing is virtue into old age,
A blessing is faith established,
A blessing is the attainment of insight-wisdom,
A blessing it is to refrain from doing wrongs.

—DHAMMAPADA 23:331–333

# Prayers and Poems

God, give us grace to accept with serenity the things
    that cannot be changed,
courage to change the things which should be
    changed,
and the wisdom to distinguish the one from the
    other.

—REINHOLD NIEBUHR,
theologian, 1892–1971

## Invictus

Out of the night that covers me,
    Black as the Pit from pole to pole,
I thank whatever gods may be
    For my unconquerable soul.

In the fell clutch of circumstance
    I have not winced nor cried aloud.

Under the bludgeonings of chance
    My head is bloody, but unbowed.

Beyond this place of wrath and tears
    Looms but the Horror of the shade,
And yet the menace of the years
    Finds, and shall find, me unafraid.

It matters not how strait the gate,
    How charged with punishments the scroll,
I am the master of my fate:
    I am the captain of my soul.

—WILLIAM ERNEST HENLEY,
poet, 1849–1903


## The Avowal

As swimmers dare
to lie face to the sky
and water bears them,
as hawks rest upon air
and air sustains them,
so would I learn to attain

freefall and float
into Creator Spirit's deep embrace,
knowing no effort earns
that all surrounding grace.

—DENISE LEVERTOV, poet, 1923–1997

# *If*

If you can keep your head when all about you
    Are losing theirs and blaming it on you,
If you can trust yourself when all men doubt you,
    But make allowance for their doubting too;
If you can wait and not be tired by waiting,
    Or being lied about, don't deal in lies,
Or being hated, don't give way to hating,
    And yet don't look too good, nor talk too wise;

If you can dream—and not make dreams your
      master;
    If you can think—and not make thoughts your
      aim;
If you can meet with Triumph and Disaster
    And treat those two imposters just the same;

If you can bear to hear the truth you've spoken
  Twisted by knaves to make a trap for fools,
Or watch the things you gave your life to, broken,
  And stoop and build 'em up with worn-out tools;

If you can make one heap of all your winnings
  And risk it on one turn of pitch-and-toss,
And lose, and start again at your beginnings
  And never breath a word about your loss;
If you can force your heart and nerve and sinew
  To serve your turn long after they are gone,
And so hold on when there is nothing in you
  Except the will which says to them: 'Hold on!'

If you can talk with crowds and keep your virtue,
  Or walk with Kings—nor lose the common touch,
If neither foes nor loving friends can hurt you,
  If all men count with you, but none too much;
If you can fill the unforgiving minute
  With sixty seconds' worth of distance run,
Yours is the Earth and everything that's in it,
  And—which is more—you'll be a Man my son!
      —RUDYARD KIPLING, author, 1865–1936

## A Psalm of Life

Tell me not, in mournful numbers,
 Life is but an empty dream!
For the soul is dead that slumbers,
 And things are not what they seem.
Life is real! Life is earnest!
 And the grave is not its goal;
Dust thou art, to dust returnest,
 Was not spoken of the soul.
Not enjoyment, and not sorrow,
 Is our destined end or way;
But to act, that each to-morrow
 Find us farther than to-day.
Art is long, and Time is fleeting,
 And our hearts, though stout and brave,
Still, like muffled drums, are beating
 Funeral marches to the grave.

In the world's broad field of battle,
 In the bivouac of Life,
Be not like dumb, driven cattle!
 Be a hero in the strife!

Trust no Future, howe'er pleasant!
    Let the dead Past bury its dead!
Act,—act in the living Present!
    Heart within, and God o'erhead!
Lives of great men all remind us
    We can make our lives sublime,
And, departing, leave behind us
    Footprints on the sands of time;
Footprints, that perhaps another,
    Sailing o'er life's solemn main,
A forlorn and shipwrecked brother,
    Seeing, shall take heart again.

Let us, then, be up and doing,
    With a heart for any fate;
Still achieving, still pursuing,
    Learn to labor and to wait.

            —HENRY WADSWORTH LONGFELLOW,
                        poet, 1807–1882

It is worthwhile for me to live
And bravely fight for saintly ideals
Although disappointed a thousand times
And perhaps even to fall in this fight
When everything would seem in vain.

Blow, angry winds, through my stony body;
You will not conquer my soul.
I have lived in the center of eternity,
My soul will be eternal.
My living was worth it.

Whoever has been set upon from all sides,
But with his soul has conquered,
Is welcome in the chorus of heroes.
Whoever has broken his shackles
And given wings to his mind
Is marching into a golden future.

—NORBERT ČAPEK, minister, 1870–1942

The world we know is passing; all things grow
  strange;
all but the stout heart's courage;
all but the undiminished lustre of an ancient
  dream—
which we shall dream again as men have dreamed
  before us,
pilgrims forever of a world forever new.

And what we loved and lost
we lose to find how great a thing
is loving
and the power of it to make a dream come true.

For us, there is no haven of refuge;
for us, there is the wilderness, wild and trackless,
where we shall build a road and sing a song.

But after us there is the Promised Land,
strong from our sorrows and shining from our joys,
our gift to those who follow us
along the road we build
singing our song.

   —A. POWELL DAVIES, minister, 1902–1957

## Memorial Day Prayer

Spirit of Life
whom we have called by many names
in thanksgiving and in anguish—

Bless the poets and those who mourn
Send peace for the soldiers who did not make the wars
but whose lives were consumed by them

Let strong trees grow above graves far from home
Breathe through the arms of their branches
The earth will swallow your tears while the dead
    sing
"No more, never again, remember me."

For the wounded ones, and those who received
    them back,
let there be someone ready when the memories come
when the scars pull and the buried metal moves
and forgiveness for those of us who were not there
for our ignorance.

And in us, veterans in a forest of a thousand fallen
    promises,
let new leaves of protest grow on our stumps.

Give us courage to answer the cry of humanity's
     pain
And with our bare hands, out of full hearts,
with all our intelligence
let us create the peace.

—BARBARA PESCAN, minister


Let me not pray to be sheltered from dangers,
But to be fearless in facing them.

Let me not beg for the stilling of my pain,
But for the heart to conquer it.

Let me not look for allies in life's battle-field,
But to my own strength.

Let me not crave in anxious fear to be saved,
But hope for the patience to win my freedom.

Grant me that I may not be a coward, feeling your
     mercy in my success alone;
But let me find the grasp of your hand in my failure.

—RABINDRANATH TAGORE, poet, 1861–1941

Great Mystery incarnate in every person and
    dwelling among us in the midst of our
    relationships, we need your help.

In a world torn by violence and fear, do not let our
    hearts be hardened.
Let us embrace those who are in need of our support.
Help us to move beyond seeking justice to seeking
    a world governed by grace.
Help us to know what needs to be done—and how
    to do it.
Where we find suffering, may we bring
    compassion.
Where we find fear, may we bring courage.
Where we find hate, may we bring love.

—Duane Finkeisen, minister


Eternal God, Mother and Father, Spirit of Life,
We are grateful for the companionship of hearts and
    minds seeking to speak the truth in love.
We are grateful for our heritage, for the women and
    men before us, whose prophetic words and deeds
    make possible our dreams and our insight.

We are grateful for the gift of life itself, mindful
   that to respect life means both to celebrate what
   it is and to insist on what it can become.
May we always rejoice in life and work to cultivate
   a sense of its giftedness, but may we also heed
   the call to transformation and growth.
May we find in ourselves the strength to face our
   adversities, the integrity to name them, and the
   vision to overcome them.
May we honor in pride the heroines and heroes of
   our past, but may we also keep company with
   the fallen, the broken, and the oppressed, for
   in the dazzling of the noonday's heat, and in
   the star-studded shimmering of night's rich
   blackness, we are they.
                    —M. SUSAN MILNOR, minister


Why do you go to the forest in search of the Divine?
God lives in all, and abides with you too.
As fragrance dwells in a flower, or reflection in a
   mirror,
so the Divine dwells inside everything;
seek therefore in your own heart.
                —TEGH BAHADUR, Sikh guru, 1621–1675

Hold on to what is good, even if it is a handful of dirt.
Hold on to what you believe, even if it is a tree that
    stands by itself.
Hold on to what you must do, even if it is a long
    way from here.
Hold on to life, even if it is easier to let go.
Hold on to my hand, even if I have gone away
    from you.

—PUEBLO BLESSING

## What God Is Like

I did not know what God is like
Until a friendly word
Came to me in an hour of need—
And it was God I heard.

I did not know what God is like
Until I heard love's feet
On errands of God's mercy
Go up and down life's street.

I did not know what God is like
Until I felt a hand

Clasp mine and lift me when alone
I had no strength to stand.

I think I know what God is like,
For I have seen the face
Of God's son looking at me
From all the human race.

—James Dillet Freeman,
minister, 1912–2003

## The Way

Friend, I have lost the way.
    The way leads on.
Is there another way?
    The way is one.
I must retrace the track.
    It's lost and gone.
Back, I must travel back!
    None goes there, none.
Then I'll make here my place—
    The road runs on—
Stand still and set my face—
    The road leaps on.

Stay here, forever stay.
 None stays here, none.
I cannot find the way.
 The way leads on.
Oh, places I have passed!
 The journey's done.
And what will come at last?
 The way leads on.

—EDWIN MUIR, poet, 1887–1959


*Nada te turbe,*
*nada te espante.*
*Quien a Dios tiene*
*nada le falta.*
*Nada te turbe,*
*nada te espante.*
*Solo Dios basta.*

No need for fear
Or deep despair
Seekers of God
Receive his care.
No need for fear

Or deep despair
We are at home
And God is there.

   —St. Teresa of Ávila, mystic, 1515–1582


God hath not promised
Skies always blue,
Flower-strewn pathways
All our lives through;
God hath not promised
Sun without rain,
Joy without sorrow,
Peace without pain.

But God hath promised
Strength for the day,
Rest for the labor,
Light for the way,
Grace for the trials,
Help from above,
Unfailing sympathy,
Undying love.

   —Annie Johnson Flint, poet, 1866–1932

## In Blackwater Woods

Look, the trees
are turning
their own bodies
into pillars

of light,
are giving off the rich
fragrance of cinnamon
and fulfillment,

the long tapers
of cattails
are bursting and floating away over
the blue shoulders

of the ponds,
and every pond
no matter what its
name is, is

nameless now.
Every year
everything
I have ever learned

in my lifetime
leads back to this: the fires
and the black river of loss
whose other side

is salvation,
whose meaning
none of us will ever know.
To live in this world

you must be able
to do three things:
to love what is mortal;
to hold it

against your bones knowing
your own life depends on it;
and, when the time comes to let it go,
to let it go.

—MARY OLIVER, poet

# Ballad of the Tempest

We were crowded in the cabin
    Not a soul would dare to sleep,—
It was midnight on the waters,
    And a storm was on the deep.

'Tis a fearful thing in winter
    To be shattered by the blast,
And to hear the rattling trumpet
    Thunder, "Cut away the mast!"

So we shuddered there in silence,—
    For the stoutest held his breath,
While the hungry sea was roaring
    And the breakers talked with death.

As thus we sat in darkness
    Each one busy with his prayers,
"We are lost!" the captain shouted,
    As he staggered down the stairs.

But his little daughter whispered,
    As she took his icy hand,
"Isn't God upon the ocean,
    Just the same as on the land?"

Then we kissed the little maiden,
    As we spake in better cheer,
And we anchored safe in harbor
    When the morn was shining clear.

—JAMES THOMAS FIELDS,
author, 1817–1881

## The Young Dead Soldiers

The young dead soldiers do not speak.
Nevertheless, they are heard in the still houses:
    who has not heard them?

They have a silence that speaks for them at night
    and when the clock counts.
They say: We were young. We have died.
    Remember us.

They say: We have done what we could but until
    it is finished it is not done.
They say: We have given our lives but until it is
    finished no one can know what our lives gave.

They say: Our deaths are not ours; they are yours;
    they will mean what you make them.

They say: Whether our lives and our deaths were
    for peace and a new hope or for nothing we
    cannot say; it is you who must say this.

They say: We leave you our deaths. Give them
    their meaning.
We were young, they say. We have died.
    Remember us.
        —ARCHIBALD MACLEISH, poet, 1892–1982


If there is to be peace in the world,
There must be peace in the nations.
If there is to be peace in the nations,
There must be peace in the cities.
If there is to be peace in the cities,
There must be peace between neighbors.
If there is to be peace between neighbors,
There must be peace in the home.
If there is to be peace in the home,
There must be peace in the heart.
        —LAO-TSE, philosopher, 5th century BCE

## During Wartime

One day, I pray,
in clear and clean windows,
reflections of families at supper,
not mouths open in fear.
One day, I pray,
in wide hot streets,
clean air, not belching oily smoke.
One day, I pray,
on warm spring nights,
the sound of crickets, not wailing or gunshots.
One day, I pray,
in human hearts,
a prayer of thanksgiving for a peace that
has lasted a hundred years;
not a truce, mind you,
but an Era of Peace full and rich and just.
May our children live to see such a world,
O Love, may all children live.
What indeed can we do?
We can breathe. We can feel heartache.
We can breathe. We can be loyal to spring.
We can breathe. We can remember the

difference between what we can do
before we have thought
and what we can do after we have thought.
We can breathe. We can remember the ways
our feelings can serve our mind.
We can breathe. We can refuse to sign
our lives over into the service of panic
or hand-wringing self-righteousness.
We can breathe. We can get clear on our
most basic values. We can breathe.
Blest are you, breath, for you are
the spirit that sustains me in difficult days.

—MARK BELLETINI, minister


Grandfather,
Look at our brokenness.

We know that in all creation
Only the human family
Has strayed from the Sacred Way.
We know that we are the ones
Who are divided,
And we are the ones
Who must come back together

To walk the Sacred Way.
Grandfather,
Sacred One,
Teach us love, compassion,
   and honor
That we may heal the earth
And heal each other.

—Ojibway prayer

## The Peace of Wild Things

When despair for the world grows in me
and I wake in the night at the least sound
in fear of what my life and my children's lives may be,
I go and lie down where the wood drake
rests in his beauty on the water, and the great heron
   feeds.

I come into the peace of wild things
who do not tax their lives with forethought
of grief. I come into the presence of still water.
And I feel above me the day-blind stars
waiting with their light. For a time
I rest in the grace of the world, and am free.

—Wendell Berry, poet

Lord, make me an instrument of Thy peace.

Where there is hatred, let me sow love,

Where there is offense, pardon,

Where there is discord, unity,

Where there is doubt, faith,

Where there is error, truth,

Where there is despair, hope,

Where there is sadness, joy,

Where there is darkness, light.

Oh, Divine Master, grant that I may not so much
    seek

To be consoled as to console,

To be understood as to understand,

To be loved as to love.

For:

It is in giving that we receive.

It is in pardoning that we are pardoned.

It is in dying that we are born to eternal life.

    —ST. FRANCIS OF ASSISI, friar, c. 1181–1226

God be in my head, and in my understanding;
God be in mine eyes and in my looking;
God be in my mouth, and in my speaking;
God be in my heart, and in my thinking;
God be at mine end, and at my departing.
Amen.

—SARUM PRIMER

# Readings

In the future days, which we seek to make secure, we look forward to a world founded upon four essential human freedoms.

The first is freedom of speech and expression—everywhere in the world.

The second is freedom of every person to worship God in his own way—everywhere in the world.

The third is freedom from want—which, translated into world terms, means economic understandings which will secure to every nation a healthy peacetime life for its inhabitants—everywhere in the world.

The fourth is freedom from fear—which, translated into world terms, means a world-wide reduction of armaments to such a point and in such a thorough fashion that no nation will be in a position to commit an act of physical aggression against any neighbor—anywhere in the world.

—FRANKLIN DELANO ROOSEVELT,
U.S. president, 1882–1945

Inevitably our anguish frames the question "Why?" if not on our lips, in our hearts. There is no answer that removes this question—no answer that can bridge the chasm of irreparable separation. Life will never be the same, and this is as it should be, for our loved ones are not expendable.

We can meet such loss only with our grief, that uncontrived mixture of courage, affirmation, and inconsolable desolation. Grief is enough; for, in our grief we live an answer, as in the depths of love and selfishness conjoin until, if we allow it, love asserts its dominance, and we become more aware of the community of living of which life makes us a part.

—PAUL N. CARNES, minister, 1921–1979

I do not pretend to understand the moral universe; the arc is a long one, my eye reaches but little ways; I cannot calculate the curve and complete the figure by the experience of sight; I can divine it by conscience. And from what I see I am sure it bends towards justice.

—THEODORE PARKER, minister, 1810–1860

The conflicts brewing today are only superficially questions of who will take power. Underneath is a deeper struggle: to change the nature of the power in which our society is rooted. The root question is, How do we define the world? For it is an old magical secret that the way we define reality shapes reality. Name a thing and you invoke it. If we call the world nonliving, we will surely kill her. But when we name the world alive, we begin to bring her back to life.

—STARHAWK, author


I have ever thought religion a concern purely between our God and our consciences, for which we were accountable to Him, and not to the priests. I never told my own religion, not scrutinized that of another. I never attempted to make a convert, nor wished to change another's creed. I have ever judged of the religion of others by their lives, for it is in our lives, and not from our words, that our religion must be read. And by the same test the world must judge me.

—THOMAS JEFFERSON,
U.S. president, 1743–1826

Religion is our human response to the dual reality of being alive and having to die. Knowing that we are going to die, we question what life means. We are not so much the animal with advanced language or the animal with tools as we are the religious animal. Having discovered relics and flowers in ancient graves, certain anthropologists apply to us the sobriquet homo religiosus. We have honored our dead from time immemorial, even as we continue to sift through their ashes in anticipation of our own earthly remains.

—FORREST CHURCH, minister, 1948–2009


In the quietness of this place, surrounded by the all-pervading Presence of God, my heart whispers: Keep fresh before me the moments of my High Resolve, that in fair weather or in foul, in good times or in tempests, in the days when the darkness and the foe are nameless or familiar, I may not forget that to which my life is committed.

Keep fresh before me
the moments of my high resolve.

—HOWARD THURMAN,
theologian, 1899–1981

To be courageous about death, we must first recognize and accept that every one of us is fearful. We are afraid that we will die, and that our loved ones will die. We are afraid that we will suffer and that we will not be ready when death comes. And we are afraid of what comes after death—if anything.

There is nothing wrong with being afraid of death, as long as we face those fears. That is courage: the ability to face what we fear instead of denying it.

—MICHAEL McGEE, minister


People say, what is the sense of our small effort.

They cannot see that we must lay one brick at a time, take one step at a time.

A pebble cast into a pond causes ripples that spread in all directions. Each one of our thoughts, words and deeds is like that.

No one has a right to sit down and feel hopeless.

There's too much work to do.

—DOROTHY DAY, activist, 1897–1980

Keep the faculty of effort alive in you by a little gratuitous exercise every day. That is, be systematically ascetic or heroic in little unnecessary points, do every day or two something for no other reason than that you would rather not do it, so that when the hour of dire need draws nigh, it may find you not unnerved and untrained to stand the test.

—WILLIAM JAMES, psychologist, 1842–1910

What words tell the truth? What balms heal? What proverbs kindle the fires and passion of joy? What spirituality stirs the hunger for justice? We seek answers to these questions—not only for ourselves, but for our communities and our society. What are the ways of being with one another that enable life to flourish, rich with meaning? When violence has fractured communities, isolated people, and broken hearts, how can life be repaired? We ask these questions not to arrive at final answers, but because asking them is fundamental to living.

—RITA NAKASHIMA BROCK, scholar, and
REBECCA ANN PARKER, minister

I believe God is everything. . . . Everything that is or ever was or ever will be. And when you can feel that, and be happy to feel that, you've found it. . . . My first step from the old white man was trees. Then air. Then birds. Then other people. But one day when I was sitting quiet and feeling like a motherless child, which I was, it come to me: that feeling of being part of everything, not separate at all. I knew that if I cut a tree, my arm would bleed. And I laughed and I cried and I run all round the house. I knew just what it was. In fact, when it happen, you can't miss it.

—ALICE WALKER, author

The line between good and evil, hope and despair, does not divide the world between "us" and "them." It runs down the middle of every one of us. I do not want to talk about what you understand about this world. I want to know what you will do about it. I do not want to know what you hope. I want to know what you will work for. I do not want your sympathy for the needs of humanity. I want your muscle. As the wagon driver said when they came to a long, hard hill, "Them that's going on with us, get out and push. Them that ain't, get out of the way."

—ROBERT FULGHUM, minister


All things in this creation exist within you, and all things in you exist in creation; there is no border between you and the closest things, and there is no distance between you and the farthest things, and all things, from the lowest to the loftiest, from the smallest to the greatest, are within you as equal things. In one atom are found all the elements of the earth; In one motion of the mind are found the motions of all the laws of existence; in one drop of water are found the secrets of all the endless oceans; in one aspect of *you* are found all the aspects of *existence*. . . . "Your life has no end, and you shall live forevermore."

—KAHLIL GIBRAN, poet, 1883–1931


We dare not forget today that we are the heirs of that first revolution. Let the word go forth from this time and place, to friend and foe alike, that the torch has been passed to a new generation of Americans—born in this century, tempered by war, disciplined by a hard and bitter peace, proud of our ancient heritage—and unwilling to witness or permit the slow undoing of those human rights to which this Nation has always been committed, and to which we are committed today, at home and around the world.

Let every nation know, whether it wishes us well or ill, that we shall pay any price, bear any burden, meet any hardship, support any friend, oppose any foe, to assure the survival and the success of liberty.

This much we pledge—and more.

—JOHN F. KENNEDY,
U.S. president, 1917–1963

Life is a tragic mystery. We are pierced and driven by laws we only half understand, we find that the lesson we learn again and again is that of accepting heroic helplessness. Some uncomprehended law holds us to a point of contradiction where we have no choice, where we do not like that which we love, where good and bad are inseparable partners impossible to tell apart, and where we—heartbroken and ecstatic, can only resolve the conflict by blindly taking it into our hearts. This used to be called being in the hands of God. Has anyone any better words to describe it?

—FLORIDA SCOTT-MAXWELL,
playwright, 1883–1979

# Reflections

Life is ever an undiscovered country. For each of us there is the first encounter with the deeper experiences of living, its grief, its pain, its joy.

—RAYMOND JOHN BAUGHAN,
minister, 1912–1993

# ACTION

*Wherever you go, preach. Use words if necessary.*
— St. Francis of Assisi, friar, c. 1181–1226

Military service is a lesson in spiritual humility. In our often self-centered culture, the military puts other things over the needs and wants of any single person. The mission comes first. What is good for the organization comes first. Our historical footprint comes first. Operational security comes first.

As service members, we are each just one cell in a huge organization that is living and breathing. It's easy to get lost as a faceless soldier, just another Joe on a mission. As people of faith, we chose a spiritual path that calls us to be greater than just another Joe. We bring compassion to those who are suffering. We offer acceptance to those who have been cast aside. We befriend those we meet, without checking out their political affiliation or religious beliefs first. We give voice to those who are overlooked and oppressed. We open our hearts and minds to spiritual wisdom from the world's religious traditions. Spiritual humility means putting ourselves aside and watching for opportunities to bring healing to a bruised and broken world. We bring healing to those around us by being the best at the role we are called to play, be it cook, clerk, medic, or infantryman.

Whatever you do, radiate your faith in your daily work and life. The smallest act of kindness, of tolerance and respect, can make waves in the life of another person. You bring peace into the world through your relationships and how you treat others.

—Rebekah Montgomery, Army chaplain

*O God, may we join the human race in daring to live in the prophetic spirit. . . . May we have communities for the whole person: truth for the mind, good works for the hands, love for the heart; and for the soul that aspiring after perfection, that unfaltering faith in life, which like lightning in the clouds, shines brightest when elsewhere it is most dark.*

*—Theodore Parker, minister, 1810–1860*

# RESTLESSNESS

*Where you go, I will go; where you lodge, I will lodge;*
*your people shall be my people, and your God my God.*
—RUTH 1:16

When people are polled about what they would do if they won the lottery, first they'd pay their bills and then they would travel—go see the world, go somewhere else and back. Nomads we are, at heart. And it always amuses me when anthropologists find the ruins of civilizations that seem to have been suddenly abandoned. What caused this? Where did they go? What was the problem? No problem really, they just woke up one morning in a collective mood to be somewhere else. They went. And just didn't quite make it back.

Count up the number of places you have lived so far in your life. Thirty-seven places in fifty-one years—that's my record—and my wife and I are talking where-to-and-what-next again. Restlessness is our way, and we scratch the itch when we can. Having traveled "somewhere else and back" quite a few times now, here are two elemental truths I know:

First: The grass is not, in fact, always greener on the other side of the fence. No, not at all. Fences have nothing to do with it. The grass is greenest where it is watered. When crossing over fences, carry water with you and tend the grass wherever you may be.

Second: The River-Runner's Maxim, taught to me when I was learning white-water canoeing. . . . "Sitting still is essential to the journey." When heading off downriver, pull over to the bank from time to time and sit quietly and look at the river and think about where you've been and where you're going and why and how.

So. Come sit by me on the bank and I will tell you where the grass is green and what I know about the river. . . .

—ROBERT FULGHUM, minister

*The journeys of our lives are never fully charted. There come to each of us deserts to cross—barren stretches—where the green edge on the horizon may be our destination, or an oasis on our way, or a mirage that beckons only to leave us lost. When fear grips the heart, or despair bows the head, may we bend, as heart and head lead us down to touch the ground beneath our feet.*

—MARGARET KEIP, minister

# SPIRIT

*Create in me a clean heart, O God, and put a new and right spirit within me.*

—PSALM 51:10

I believe that Spirit is one and is everywhere present. That it never leaves me. That in my ignorance I may withdraw from it, but I can realize its presence the instant I return to my senses.

It is this belief in a power larger than myself and other than myself which allows me to venture into the unknown and even the unknowable. I cannot separate what I conceive as Spirit from my concept of God. I believe that God is Spirit.

While I know myself as a creation of God, I am also obligated to realize and remember that everyone else and everything else are also God's creation. This is particularly difficult for me when my mind falls upon the cruel person, the batterer, and the bigot. I would like to think that the mean-spirited were created by another force and under the aegis and direction of something other than my God. But since I believe that God created all things, I am not only constrained to know that the oppressor is a child of God, but also obliged to try to treat him or her as a child of God.

My faith is tested many times every day, and more times than I'd like to confess, I'm unable to keep the banner of faith aloft. If a promise is not kept, or if a secret is betrayed, or if I experience long-lasting pain, I begin to doubt God and God's love. I fall so miserably into the chasm of disbelief that I cry out in despair. Then the Spirit lifts me up again, and once more I am secured in faith. I don't know how that happens, save when I cry out earnestly I am answered immediately and am returned to faithfulness. I am once again filled with the Spirit and firmly planted on solid ground.

—MAYA ANGELOU, author

*Spirit of Life and Love, strengthen our resolve to live out our faith. Fill us with the spirit, which will give us both courage and strength to move out into the world, and there, to make a difference. By our efforts, may your will be done. Amen.*

—SYDNEY K. WILDE, minister

# PRAYER

*Pray without ceasing.*

—1 THESSALONIANS 5:17

My mother, devout in her faith, prayed without ceasing for decades. First thing in the morning and last thing in the evening, she would lift up her family, friends, neighborhood, nation, and world to God. She walked through the world always recognizing God's presence and thanking God for the many blessings in her life and in others' lives. I was always comforted knowing that she prayed for me and others—without ceasing.

Years after her death, I went through a challenging time and experienced great suffering. My heart and spirit sank deeply, and I wished I could turn to mother for her prayers. The only prayer I could utter myself was "Help." Eventually, I remembered an experience I had while traveling in Greece years earlier. At dinner, my host family would pray for the local monks. They explained that they prayed for the monks because the monks were praying for them and for all people. Ceaseless prayer is at the heart of monastic life. It serves as a reminder that all the monks do is focused on the presence of God.

This memory was an answer to my prayer. I felt heartened by the monks' ceaseless prayers. I knew again that someone, even if it was someone I would never know, was praying for me. My heart and spirit rose, and I offered the only prayer possible: "Thank you."

Sometimes prayer is just that simple—"help" and "thank you." An answer always comes. It may or may not be the answer we want. Whatever the answer, may we continue to practice surrendering our will to God's, recalling the words of the fourteenth-century German philosopher Meister Eckhart: "If the only prayer you ever say in your entire life is thank you, it will be enough."

May it be so.

—CYNTHIA L. G. KANE, Navy chaplain

*God, help us to pray without ceasing, just as we remember that someone is praying for our comfort, healing, and wholeness. May we always be called to extend a caring hand and to accept the one extended to us.*

—EDS.

# HUMILITY

*Blessed are the meek, for they will inherit the earth.*
—MATTHEW 5:5

After my father passed away in 2006, we went through his things. He was always so full of life and his belongings spoke of his adventures. I found photos of him as a young man playing an accordion, as a middle-aged man dressed in a Santa suit (he loved playing Santa), and as an older man, clutching a stuffed bear bigger than he was. In another photo, taken on his eightieth birthday, he was riding a roller coaster with a bunch of twentysomethings, and he had this great big grin on his face. . . .

My dad had also saved a stack of papers. There were letters regarding his insurance business and documents about his charitable projects. Then, buried in the stack, we found a citation issued in 1945, when my father was in the army. The citation for "heroic achievement" came from the commanding general of the 75th Infantry Division.

On April 11, 1945, my father's infantry company was attacked by German forces, and in the early stages of battle, heavy artillery fire led to eight casualties. According to the citation: "With complete disregard for his own safety, Private Pausch leaped from a covered position and commenced treating the wounded men while shells continued to fall in the immediate vicinity. So successfully did this soldier administer medical attention that all the wounded were evacuated successfully."

In recognition for this, my dad, then twenty-two years old, was issued the Bronze Star for valor.

In the fifty years my parents were married, in the thousands of conversations my dad had with me, it had just never come up. And so there I was, weeks after his death, getting another lesson from him about the meaning of sacrifice—and about the power of humility.

—RANDY PAUSCH, professor, 1960–2008

*God of all creation, bless all who serve. Be with them in harm's way, throughout their lives, and on into death, that their memory, their sacrifice, and their service may teach those who follow.*

—EDS.

# JOURNEYS

*When I was a child, I spoke like a child, I thought like a child, I reasoned like a child; when I became an adult, I put an end to childish ways. For now we see in a mirror, dimly, but then we will see face to face. Now I know only in part; then I will know fully, even as I have been fully known.*

—1 CORINTHIANS 13:11–12

Why did you join the military? Was it duty, honor, and country? Economic necessity? To leave behind childish ways? To get as far away from home as possible? To see the world? Most likely, you are serving for a combination of some or all of these and many other reasons. The burden and privilege of military service is the opportunity and responsibility to travel—sometimes to hell and back in harm's way, sometimes to the world's most magnificent vistas, sometimes to its loneliest and most remote corners. We are world travelers, for better and for worse. We experience that which others never will, for better and for worse. We grow up in the process, for better and for worse. At first we see in a mirror dimly, but then face to face, for better and for worse.

Too often as we venture out into the world—in all of its triumph and tragedy, joy and sorrow, heaven and hell—we risk severing our roots. We lose touch with our reasons for being and serving. We drift further away from our families and loved ones. We change more than we want or they expect, and we return home. In the end, we have to return home. And we will venture out again. As T.S. Eliot tells us, "We shall not cease from exploration."

—EDS.

*Spirit of life, give us strength to serve, to accept the burden and privilege of risking our lives for others' safety and freedom. Be with us on each journey that we may also be safe, that we may be more fully known, and may return to our loved ones, seeing, loving, and knowing them more fully.*

—EDS.

# GOOD WORKS

*So faith by itself, if it has no works, is dead.*

—JAMES 2:17

In our modern age of apathy and egoism, there is cause for hope whenever people care about something beyond themselves. But there is more to being human than feeling deeply, for we risk becoming impassioned fools. Our minds must conspire with our hearts. We should care enough to think—and think with great care.

No human endeavor shows the double-edged nature of caring like religion, with its boundless capacity to foster our humanity and its vulnerability to thoughtless passion. In a world of suffering, a moral life means not merely believing the right things but doing good works.

What does it mean that Jesus was divine, if we treat the homeless man in the alley as less than human?

What does it mean for God to be all powerful, if we don't use our power to help others?

What does it mean that the Bible was divinely inspired, if we write laws that are profane?

What does it mean for there to be a heaven, if the hell of violence burns next door?

What does it mean that Mary was a virgin, if we do not heed the cries of a woman being raped or abused?

What does it mean to be "saved," when a child loses all hope?

What does it mean for God to have declared that Creation was good, if seventy species disappear every day?

Many people care about religious matters, but James asks us, "What is the good of that?" If our beliefs have meaning—if we care about divinity, God's power, ancient wisdom, heaven, miraculous birth, salvation, and all of Creation—we must act as if our souls depend on it. As Gandhi taught, you must be the change you want to see in the world. Let us build a life in which our work speaks for our faith.

—JEFFREY LOCKWOOD, professor

*God of heaven, eternal spirit, help me to care about things that matter most. My tears are for the homeless, the helpless, the hopeless, the abused and violated. I care about the divine because I care about them.*

—EDS.

# AFFIRMATION

*You are a child of God. Your playing small does not serve the world.*

—MARIANNE WILLIAMSON, author

It's time somebody told you that you are lovely, good and real; that your beauty can make hearts stand still. It's time somebody told you how much they love and need you, how much your spirit helped set them free, how your eyes shine full of light. It's time somebody told you.

It's time someone told you that with all your flaws and weaknesses, you are an extraordinary person, well-worth knowing. No one—especially not God or the people who love you—expects you to live without making mistakes or stumbling occasionally. It's time you looked at your own life with more kindness, gentleness, and mercy.

It's time someone told you that you are not on this earth to impress anyone, to dazzle us with your success, to conquer all obstacles with your competence, or to offer one brilliant solution after another. We are happy you are here with the rest of us struggling souls. We are all striving to be as faithful as we can be to the truth that we understand. No more is required.

It's time someone told you that the work you do to increase your capacity to love and to pay attention is more important than any other activity. As you advance closer to what is ultimately true and life-giving, you bless others.

It's time somebody told you how absolutely beautiful your laughter is. You bring joy into our world.

Just possibly, messages of love and acceptance have always been circulating in our midst. The hard part is not seeking out these positive and creative affirmations that remind us that we are loved. The hard part is taking in the love.

It's time someone told us all that we are valued and infinitely worthwhile.

And it's time we believed it.

—BARBARA MERRITT, minister

*Save us, our compassionate Lord, from our folly, by your wisdom, from our arrogance, by your forgiving love, from our greed, by your infinite bounty, and from our insecurity by your healing power.*

—MUSLIM PRAYER

# FREEDOM

*Free at last! free at last! thank God Almighty, we are free at last!*

—MARTIN LUTHER KING JR.,
minister, 1929–1968

Independence Day is a day of family gatherings, cookouts, games, parades, and fireworks. We pay tribute to those who created this country in the name of life, liberty, and the pursuit of happiness. We honor those who have served our country. We celebrate the unmatched freedom and good fortune that we enjoy in the United States of America.

And yet, we need to remember that our freedom was bought at a cost much deeper than the sacrifices of our nation's founders and fallen soldiers. Americans enjoy their freedom also at the expense of those indigenous peoples who were killed or corralled onto reservations. We enjoy these freedoms partially at the hands of slave labor in the founding century after independence. All men and women may have been created equal, but they have seldom been treated equally.

We may never achieve a utopian society where freedom rings on every front for every person. But freedom will not ring for anyone unless we work continuously for it. Our society and our freedoms are built on a system of checks and balances, on questioning, on a healthy tradition of doubt and inquiry. We must question the status quo, not always to defeat it but to ensure that good intentions have positive results.

Our nation and the world are on the verge of a new era, a new global reality that will define our future and that of our children and their children. We are a global village, but we have not learned to live in global peace and justice. If we are to live in a safe world, free not only of terrorism but of intolerance, injustice, oppression, and inequality, we need to reject the path of least resistance in favor of that which embraces the unexplainable, which gives meaning to our lives.

Let freedom ring.

—Eds.

*God of many names, gives us the strength to defend freedom in all of its forms. Help us to be mindful of the costs of freedom. Remind us to be constant in insisting upon freedom for all.*

—Eds.

# COMMITMENT

*Never doubt that a small group of thoughtful, committed citizens can change the world; indeed it's the only thing that ever has.*

—MARGARET MEAD, activist

The American commitment is to universal justice, the rights of all people, not the special interests of some. It is a commitment to fair play, to patience, to tolerance, to neighborliness. It is a commitment to the common good. It protects liberty with unity, the opportunity of each with the good of all. It is compassionate, humanitarian. It believes in humanity and in its future. It is the Golden Rule. It is based upon the claim of conscience and the faith in goodness. It begins not in a system but within the heart.

It battles prejudice and false opinion. It seeks the truth. It is opposed to barriers of exclusiveness. Its principles are universal. It despises cowardice, including moral cowardice. But it also has no use for obstinacy, inflexibility, and intolerance. It prefers honesty to cleverness, kindness to self-sufficiency, goodwill to narrow-minded aims. It is a way of life now and a faith, a vision of the future. It is a purpose to be served.

If anyone asks by what right I define these characteristics as American, I point him to those Americans the rest of us revere as great. I say that America is defined by the moral progress she has sought, and by exemplars, not by the hour of perfidy and by her little-minded, greedy foes.

And if anyone tells me that these characteristics are more than American, that they are universal, I will reply that that is why they are American. Because this nation was *not* founded on the divisive and separate, but upon the rights of all people. Can we restore these standards? Can we seek again the touch of greatness?

The future will depend upon the answer. Upon what takes place in heart and conscience. A nation, like an individual, must have a soul.

—A. POWELL DAVIES, minister, 1902–1957

*May we—through our commitments to universal justice; to the rights of all people; to fair play, patience, and tolerance; and to the common good—give soul to this nation we love.*

—EDS.

# DEATH

*Though an army encamp against me, my heart shall not*
*fear; though war rise up against me, yet I will be confident.*

—PSALM 27:3

War threatens us with death and pain. No man . . .
need try to attain a stoic indifference about these
things, but we can guard against the illusions of the
imagination. We think of the streets of Warsaw and
contrast the deaths there suffered with an abstraction
called Life. But there is no question of death or life
for any of us, only a question of this death or of that—
of a machine gun bullet now or a cancer forty years
later. What does war do to death? It certainly does
not make it more frequent: 100 percent of us die, and
the percentage cannot be increased. It puts several
deaths earlier, but I hardly suppose that that is what
we fear. Certainly when the moment comes, it will
make little difference how many years we have behind
us. Does it increase our chances of a painful death? I
doubt it. As far as I can find out, what we call natural
death is usually preceded by suffering, and a battlefield

is one of the very few places where one has a reasonable prospect of dying with no pain at all. Does it decrease our chances of dying at peace with God? I cannot believe it. If active service does not persuade a man to prepare for death, what conceivable concatenation of circumstances would? Yet war does do something to death. It forces us to remember it. . . . War makes death real to us, and that would have been regarded as one of its blessings by most of the great Christians of the past.

—C. S. Lewis, theologian, 1898–1963

*Teach me your way, O Lord, and lead me on a level path because of my enemies. Do not give me up to the will of my adversaries, for false witnesses have risen against me, and they are breathing out violence.*

—Psalm 27:11–12

# CYCLES

*All streams run to the sea, but the sea is not full; to the place where the streams flow, there they continue to flow.*
—ECCLESIASTES 1:7

Intermittency—an impossible lesson for human beings to learn. How can one learn to live through the ebb-tides of one's existence? How can one learn to take the trough of the wave? It is easier to understand here on the beach, where the breathlessly still ebb-tides reveal another life below the level which mortals usually reach. In this crystalline moment of suspense, one has a sudden revelation of the secret kingdom at the bottom of the sea. Here in the shallow flats one finds, wading through warm ripples, great horse-conchs pivoting on a leg; white sand dollars, marble medallions engraved in the mud; and myriads of bright-colored cochina-clams, glistening in the foam, their shells opening and shutting like butterflies' wings. So beautiful is the still hour of the sea's withdrawal, as beautiful as the sea's return when the encroaching waves pound up the beach, pressing to reach those dark rumpled chains of seaweed which mark the last high tide.

Perhaps this is the most important thing for me to take back from beach-living: simply the memory that each cycle of the tide is valid; each cycle of the wave is valid; each cycle of a relationship is valid. And my shells? I can sweep them all into my pocket. They are only there to remind me that the sea recedes and returns eternally.

—ANNE MORROW LINDBERGH,
aviator, 1906–2001

*Thou art as the sea, and we but small bays. We cannot hold Thee. Yet may Thy tides run through us and fill us with some intimation of the sea from which strength comes.*
—RAYMOND JOHN BAUGHAN, 1912–1993

# MEMORIAL DAY

*Day is done, gone the sun,*
*From the lake, from the hills, from the sky.*
*All is well, safely rest, God is nigh.*

—Daniel Butterfield,
Union General, 1831–1901

There are many stories about the beginning of Memorial Day. The first official observance was on May 30, 1868, when flowers were placed on the graves of Union and Confederate soldiers at Arlington National Cemetery. Since World War I, Memorial Day has been commemorated as a day to honor all men and women who have died while serving in our nation's military.

On Memorial Day, our nation pauses to express its appreciation to those who have served and who continue to serve in our nation's armed forces.

On Memorial Day, we remember our comrades in uniform whom we have loved and lost in service to our nation. We express gratitude for their lives and their sacrifices even as we risk our own.

On Memorial Day, no matter our feelings about war, we remember the sacrifices made. May we honor the lives of those who have died, and may we reach out in love to our living veterans and their families, extending the olive branch of acceptance and respect as our faith calls us to each and every day.

War is a horror. May we never use Memorial Day as a time to glorify militarism or the killing and destructiveness of this human aberration we call war. We yearn for peace, and we pray for the day when nations pursue understanding over violence in resolving disputes.

—FLOYD VERNON CHANDLER,
Army chaplain

*In the Holy Quiet of this hour, their names surround us and they live with us in blessed memory. May we remain together in silence, as a tribute to all that they have meant to us.*

—WAYNE B. ARNASON, minister

# COURAGE

*Courage is what preserves our liberty, safety, life, and our homes and parents, our country and children. Courage comprises all things.*

—PLAUTUS, playwright, 254–184 BCE

When each of us enlisted or was commissioned, we swore an oath to "support and defend the Constitution of the United States against all enemies, foreign and domestic" and "to bear true faith and allegiance to the same." This is an oath of devotion to our country. Those of us in uniform are required to exhibit unwavering loyalty, no matter the circumstances. Every good soldier, sailor, airman, and marine knows this. But we also quickly learn that the task of defending our nation against "all enemies" requires a great deal of courage. We sometimes think that courage is only the stuff of battlefields and combat, but "courage comprises all things."

Courage is not only necessary in harm's way. It sustains us through every aspect of life. For example, it reaches its highest point when a service member must leave a child in the care of others because they have been deployed to far-off lands. This incredible sacrifice takes almost unfathomable courage. It is perhaps the ultimate sacrifice for country. The personal toll on both service member and family is tremendous, but justified by the freedom of others to be with their families. This sacrifice merits profound gratitude.

—EDS.

*Spirit of Life, grant us the courage to serve and help us to know that we are fulfilling a higher purpose. Protect us so that we may return to family once again. Protect our families and give them the courage to remain strong until we return to their loving arms.*

—EDS.

# FAITH

*We are not to do, but to let do; not to work, but to be worked upon; and to this homage there is a consent of all thoughtful and just men in all ages and conditions.*

—RALPH WALDO EMERSON,
philosopher, 1803–1882

Many people have defined faith. Some offer a definition with religious connotations, while others focus on the word's universal meaning. For military members, faith has a broader set of meanings concerned with protecting democracy and trusting our leaders. We offer service to our country in good faith, and hope that our service will bring about a common good. However one defines faith, it is about maintaining hope in future outcomes.

The Transcendentalist philosopher Ralph Waldo Emerson speaks of the open-ended nature of faith. He says that, at its core, faith cannot be shaped or made but occurs in us as we trust in what is to come. We trust that we will have the strength and courage to meet the challenges that we encounter now and those that lie ahead.

Faith preempts our need to know. Faith is about letting and being. We release ourselves to let experience happen so that we may be our best selves. While this means giving up the need to control every aspect of our lives, we do not stand still. We keep moving into the future with a conviction that our service is honorable and contributes to noble ends: love of fellow human beings, service beyond self, and peace throughout the world. If not now, in the future we anticipate.

So, let us march forward, standing firm on our faith. Let us trust that outcomes will be good and just. Let us do—and be worked upon.

—XOLANI KACELA, Air Force chaplain

*Divine Spirit, strengthen our faith. Help us to be trusting and courageous in the face of doubt and uncertainty. May we have faith and confidence in you, in ourselves, and in our vital mission.*

—EDS.

# BELIEF

*Be ye lamps unto yourselves; be your own confidence.*
*Hold to the truth within yourselves as to the only lamp.*
—THE BUDDHA

At a recent funeral, the officiating clergy person, knowing that many present were not adherents of his particular faith and belief, provided some explanation regarding certain beliefs, symbols, and rituals. This was a bit unusual for a funeral, and some found it patronizing, but he did not mean it to be. He was truly trying to reach out and bridge a gap, even if awkwardly.

The real issue arose when he spoke for "non-believers." He said something like, "When we die, non-believers think it is lights out. Believers look to a new life." He was trying to explain the symbolism of baptism and resurrection.

Many people do not believe in a specific theology or deity, or participate in a religious community. But this does not stop them from being devoted people of faith. Many "non-believers" even believe that life is eternal—not necessarily in the sense that there is a heaven but in that we leave a legacy behind. We live on in the memories and deeds of those whose lives we affected while we were here. We leave behind our deeds. Those who follow us leave theirs, and so on. We can create heaven or hell here on earth. We can leave behind positive, negative, or irrelevant memories and legacies for eternity to deal with. All of our lights shine on forever, for better or worse.

—Eds.

*In the presence of those we love, in remembrance of those who have gone before us, and in anticipation of those yet to enter our lives, may we have the strength, wisdom, and courage to be our best selves, to let our lights shine so that others may benefit from our small effort.*

—Eds.

# RESPECT

*God shows no partiality.*

—ROMANS 2:11

As military members, we are constantly urged to respect others. Paying respect includes recognizing and acknowledging rank, following rules against fraternizing, saluting the American flag, and honoring our brothers and sisters who have given their lives serving our country. In many ways, ours is a vocation grounded in respect.

We are also spiritual beings, in touch with an ultimate reality that knows us deep in our souls. In terms of respect, scripture says that God treats us all impartially. In the words of Luke, each of us receives an equal measure of God's love, care, and compassion that is "pressed down, shaken together, running over." We respond by treating others the same way. Respect is one way that we fulfill our spiritual vocation of spreading love across the land.

Respect can be difficult to embrace in war, during state and national emergencies, and when confronting personal issues, losses, and tragedies. It can be difficult when we interact with people who have different faith traditions and beliefs than ours. But difficulties do not diminish the truth that God loves all people. It is easy to believe that God is only on our side, and that we, therefore, deserve preference over others. We counter this mindset by remembering that respect flows from humility, a universally accepted spiritual practice.

As we go into the world, let us be mindful that to get respect, we must show respect. Just as God loves us all equally, we should offer no less to our families, friends, co-workers, and leaders, even those across enemy lines.

—Xolani Kacela, Air Force chaplain

*Almighty, help us to be respectful of others and to treat one another with compassion. As we embrace a spirit of care and respect, we pray that peace will engulf the land.*

—Eds.

# RESPONSIBILITY

*Those who deny freedom to others deserve it not for themselves, and cannot long retain it.*

—ABRAHAM LINCOLN,
U.S. president, 1809–1865

In the United States, we enjoy freedoms unknown in many corners of the world, and we have all heard the saying that "Freedom is not free." One of the costs is sacrifice on the part of those who serve in the military. Obligation and responsibility come with freedom. James Luther Adams said, "Only the society that creates social forms of freedom in a community of justice (where every man is given his due), only the freedom that respects the divine image and dignity in every man, are dependable." Martin Luther King Jr. called this the Beloved Community, a completely integrated society, a community of love and justice, in which freedom and brotherhood/sisterhood are realities.

As military personnel, how do we both safeguard the freedoms of those we protect and live up to our obligation to respect the divine spark in every human being, even those against whom we must fight? Military service requires us to engage in warfare, violence, and killing, but it does not mandate that we engage in abuse or torture. It does not require us to destroy more than is necessary to achieve our objectives. It does not require us to deprive our enemies of their rights or dignity as human beings. In fact, we are obligated to act with mercy and compassion toward our defeated, wounded, and captured enemies. Even through military service, each of us can fulfill our religious and moral responsibility to advance the cause of justice and freedom, to help build the Beloved Community on Earth.

—TOM BEALL, veteran

*In the Name of Allah, the beneficent, the merciful: Praise be to the Lord of the Universe who has created us and made us into tribes and nations that we may know each other, not that we may despise each other. If the enemy incline towards peace, do thou also incline towards peace, and trust in God, for the Lord is one that hears and knows all things. And the servants of God Most Gracious are those who walk on the Earth in humility, and when we address them, we say "Peace."*

—QUR'AN 4:90

# BROKENNESS

*The world breaks every one and afterward many are stronger at the broken places.*
— ERNEST HEMINGWAY, author, 1899–1961

No one survives this world without wounds and pains, without loss and grief. No one walks this earth without failure, without falling, without being less than they might have been.

And yet, our ability to break keeps us alive. Our capacity to admit when we are hurt, when we are afraid, when we have lost something precious, and when we have lost hope gives us the opportunity to become stronger. Unlike our bones when we are physically hurt, our souls and spirits grow stronger than they were before the injury. Painful places become powerful. Empty places become full.

We achieve this healing not through a miracle but by sharing our pain, anguish, and hurt with one another. We tell each other our stories, just as warriors have after battle for thousands of years. We tell of how we miss those who are gone, of how we regret the place where we failed, of how we were afraid. We remember lost comrades. We remember lost hopes. We remember dreams that seem far away.

Through that sharing, we learn that we are not alone. Our failures and wounds bind us together in ways no success ever can. A failure shared is no longer lonely. A loss shared is a something precious found again. A pain shared is a pain eased. In sharing with one another, we become strong in the broken places.

—DAVID PYLE, Army chaplain

*God of our hearts, when we feel heartache, when the pain is too great, when we fail, when hope fades, when we are broken, battered, and bloody, may we find strength in sharing and knowing that we are not alone.*

—EDS.

# STILLNESS

*Be still, and know that I am God!*
*I am exalted among the nations, I am exalted in the earth.*
—PSALM 46:10

Some may call it a command, but it might be better
to hear this psalm as an invitation to simply be still.
So often the pace of life seems impossible to main-
tain, at least not at the level that is expected of a war-
rior. Between the call to duty, service to country, care
for family, and other responsibilities, making time to
be still can seem unthinkable.

Yet, it is in stillness that God is most present.
Without stillness, it's hard to gain the wisdom or be
fueled by the spirit and strength that are necessary for
daily life. Without stillness, there is only hurry, angst,
exhaustion, and stress. Without stillness, there is no
hope, no peace, no semblance of balance.

As warriors, as citizens, as sons and daughters,
mothers and fathers, brothers and sisters, as everyday
people striving to live right, we do well to accept the
invitation to stillness, to receive and honor it as a gift.

In just a few minutes each day, we can find the stillness necessary to experience the divine. With daily practice, the divine becomes part of our own living and being. We must be still to know God.

—KELLY E. CUMMINS-PICKENS,
Army chaplain

*Find a stillness, hold a stillness, let the stillness carry me.*
*In the spirit, by the spirit, with the spirit giving power,*
*I will find true harmony.*

—CARL SEABURG, minister, 1922–1998

# GRACE

*For by grace you have been saved through faith, and this is not your own doing, it is the gift of God.*

—EPHESIANS 2:8

I believe any discussion of Grace must begin with a theology of random events—with a belief that whatever comes from a particular event in our lives is not foreordained, predestined, calculated, meaning-laden, lesson-ripe—it just is. Whatever comes will come as the events continue to unfold, and our job is to pay attention.

It would be nice to believe that things that happen to us are personalized. That even the tragedies of our lives are shaped for us because we need them. It might redeem them, somehow. But I don't believe that. Grace, if there is grace, begins with the recognition that loss can be very real.

Grace is what comes to you beyond what you expected—often in spite of what you expected. It is most often seen in the surprise of life, in wonder, in a sudden unfolding of new life. It comes in the midst of our plans, changing them and letting us know, once again, that it is *not* all up to us.

Grace, the gift of God/Life/the Forces among us—whatever you call it—comes in ways we can't manage, in response to prayers we can't utter, in the midst of situations that give us no guarantees. Grace is a deep existential trust that we reach, not by plan or even intention but in recognition of that which emerges from the depths of our beings to sustain us.

How do you know if you have been visited by grace? When you experience an overwhelming sense of gratitude, even in the difficulty of pain and tragedy. When you realize that we are all in one boat in spite of our need to grasp at straws and *make* things work.

—LAUREL HALLMAN, minister

*Through many dangers, toils, and snares, I have already*
*come.*
*'Tis grace that brought me safe thus far*
*And grace will lead me home.*

—JOHN NEWTON, clergyman, 1725–1805

# FORGIVENESS

*Then Peter came and said to him, Lord, "if another member of the church sins against me, how often should I forgive? As many as seven times?" Jesus said to him, "Not seven times, but, I tell you, seventy-seven times."*

—MATTHEW 18:21–22

There's a transformational story in the Gospel according to Luke. Jesus is teaching. His listeners include people from Galilee, Judea, and Jerusalem. There is standing room only, and the door is blocked. Some men have brought a paralyzed friend, in his bed, to be healed, but the crowd is so big that they can't get him through the door to see Jesus. The people don't make way to let this stranger through. And so the men carry their friend to the roof and lower his bed through the ceiling tiles so that he can see Jesus. When Jesus sees their faith, he says, "Friend, your sins are forgiven you," but the Pharisees in the crowd question Jesus' authority to grant forgiveness. Jesus replies, "Which is easier, to say, 'Your sins are forgiven you,' or to say 'Stand up and walk'?" Then he turns to the paralyzed man and says, "I say to you, stand up and take your bed and go away to your home."

We needn't take this story to mean that the man's paralysis is related to his sins. But the story does draw a mysterious connection between forgiveness and healing. We become broken when we find ourselves isolated from each other. Loving community is built on the premise that we can all relieve our pain by forgiving each other, and allowing ourselves to be forgiven, for the inevitable injuries and traumas that human beings inflict on each other, even unintentionally.

Forgiveness has been called "letting go of all hope for a different yesterday." Indeed, we cannot change the past. But until we forgive those who made the past other than we hoped it would be, we cannot move forward to the future we imagine.

—Eds.

*For dismissing others when we could have embraced them, for failing to forgive those who made the past different than we had dreamed, for isolating ourselves from each other and the divine, may we too be forgiven.*

—Eds.

# Hymns

## Vine and Fig Tree

♩=116

**1** And ev-'ry one 'neath a vine and fig tree shall live in peace and un-a-fraid. And ev-'ry fraid.

**2** And in-to plow-shares turn their swords, na-tions shall learn war no more. war no more.

Words: Micah 4:3-4
Music: Traditional Hebrew

# Where Do We Come From?

Where do we come from? What are we?

Where are we go - ing?

Where do we come from?

Mys - te - ry. Mys - te - ry.

Life is a rid-dle and a mys - te - ry.

Where do we come from? Where are we go - ing?

Words: Paul Gauguin & Brian Tate, © 1999 Brian Tate
Music: Brian Tate, © 1999 Brian Tate

# Mother Spirit, Father Spirit

♩=72

1. Moth-er Spir-it, Fa-ther Spir-it, where are
2. Man-y drops are in the o-cean, deep and
3. I am emp-ty, time flies from me; what is
4. Moth-er Spir-it, Fa-ther Spir-it, take our

you? In the sky song, in the for-est,
wide. Sun-light bounc-es off the rip-ples
time? Dreams e-ter-nal, fears in-fer-nal
hearts. Take our breath and let our voic-es

sounds your cry. What to give you,
to the sky. What to give you,
haunt my heart. What to give you,
sing our parts. Take our hands and

what to call you, what am I?
what to call you, who am I?
what to call you, O, my God?
let us work to shape our art.

Original words & music: Norbert F. Capek
English version: Richard Frederick Boeke

# Come, Come, Whoever You Are

Come, come, who - ev - er you

are, wan - der - er, wor - ship - er,

lov - er of leav - ing. Ours is no

car - a - van of____ de - spair.

Come, yet a - gain come.____

Words: adapted from Jalaluddin Rumi
Music: Lynn Adair Ungar, © 1989 Lynn Adair Ungar

# Guide My Feet

1. Guide my feet while I run this race.
2. Hold my hand while I run this race.
3. Stand by me while I run this race.
4. Search my heart while I run this race.

Guide my feet while I run this race, for I
Hold my hand
Stand by me
Search my heart

Guide my feet
Hold my hand
Stand by me
Search my heart

Guide my
Hold my
Stand by
Search my

don't want to run this race in vain! *(race in vain!)*

Words & music: Traditional

# We Are Climbing Jacob's Ladder

1. We are climb-ing Ja-cob's
2. Ev-'ry round goes high-er,
3. If I stum-ble, will you
4. Though the road is steep and

lad-der, we are climb-ing
high-er, ev-'ry round goes
help me? If I stum-ble,
rug-ged, though the road is

Ja-cob's lad-der, we are
high-er, high-er, ev-'ry
will you help me? If I
steep and rug-ged, though the

climb-ing Ja-cob's lad-der,
round goes high-er, high-er,
stum-ble, will you help me?
road is steep and rug-ged,

we are climb-ing on.
we are climb-ing on.
We are climb-ing on.
we are climb-ing on.

Words & music: Traditional

98

# One More Step

1. One more step,
2. One more word,
3. One more prayer,
4. One more song,

we will take one more
we will say one more
we will say one more
we will sing one more

step, 'til there is peace for
word, 'til ev - ery word is
prayer, 'til ev - ery prayer is
song, 'til ev - ery song is

us and ev - ery - one, we'll take
heard by ev - ery - one, we'll say
shared by ev - ery - one, we'll say
sung by ev - ery - one, we'll sing

one more step.
one more word.
one more prayer.
one more song.

Words & music: Joyce Poley, © 1986 Joyce Poley

# Winds Be Still

Words: Richard S. Kimball, © 1986 Tirik Productions
Music: Samuel Sebastian Wesley

# Voice Still and Small

Words & music: John Corrado, © 1987 John Corrado

# Meditation on Breathing

Words & music: Sarah Dan Jones, © 2001 Sarah Dan Jones

# I Saw Three Ships

1. I saw three ships come sail - ing in, On
2. And what was in those ships all three, On
3. The Vir - gin Mary and Christ were there, On
4. Pray, whith - er sailed those ships all three, On

Christ - mas day, on Christ - mas day; I
Christ - mas day, on Christ - mas day? And
Christ - mas day, on Christ - mas day; The
Christ - mas day, on Christ - mas day? Pray,

saw three ships come sail - ing in, On
what was in those ships all three, On
Vir - gin Mary and Christ were there, On
whith - er sailed those ships all three, On

Christ - mas day in the morn - ing.
Christ - mas day in the morn - ing?
Christ - mas day in the morn - ing.
Christ - mas day in the morn - ing?

5. O they sailed into Bethlehem,
On Christmas day, on Christmas day;
O they sailed into Bethlehem,
On Christmas day in the morning.

6. And all the bells on earth shall ring,
On Christmas day, on Christmas day;
And all the bells on earth shall ring,
On Christmas day in the morning.

7. And all the souls on earth shall sing,
On Christmas day, on Christmas day;
And all the souls on earth shall sing,
On Christmas day in the morning.

8. Then let us all rejoice amain,
On Christmas day, on Christmas day;
Then let us all rejoice amain,
On Christmas day in the morning.

Words & music: Traditional

# When Will the Fighting Cease?

*Translation of Latin: Give peace, Lord, in our time.*

Words: Nick Page & Nita Penfold, © 2002 Nick Page
Music: Melchior Franck

# Spirit of Life

Spir - it of Life, come un - to me.
Sing in my heart all the stir - rings of com -
pas - sion. Blow in the wind, rise in the
sea; move in the hand, giv - ing
life the shape of jus - tice. Roots hold me
close; wings set me free;
Spir - it of Life, come to me, come to me.

Words & music: Carolyn McDade, © 1981 Carolyn McDade

# Fuente de Amor

Fuen - te de_A - mor, ven ha - cia mí.

Y_al co - ra - zón, cán - ta - le tu com - pa -

sión.___ So - pla_al vo - lar, su - be_en la

mar, has - ta mol - dear la jus -

ti - cia de la vi - da. A - rrái - ga -

me, li - bé - ra - me,

Fuen - te de_A - mor, ven a mí, ven a mí.

Original words & music: Carolyn McDade, © 1981 Carolyn McDade
Spanish version: Ervin Barrios, © 1999 Ervin Barrios

Unitarian Universalism is a non-creedal, liberal religion with Jewish-Christian roots. It affirms the inherent worth of all people; advocates freedom of belief and the search for advancing truth; and aims to provide a warm, open, supportive community for people who believe that ethical living is the supreme witness of religion.

The largest Unitarian Universalist congregation is the Church of the Larger Fellowship, which provides a web-based ministry for those unable to attend a Unitarian Universalist church.

The primary expression of Unitarian Universalist values is our Principles, which affirm and promote the inherent worth and dignity of every person; justice, equity, and compassion in human relations; acceptance of one another and encouragement to spiritual growth in our congregations; a free and responsible search for truth and meaning; the right of conscience and the use of the democratic process within our congregations and in society at large; the goal of world community with peace, liberty, and justice for all; and respect for the interdependent web of all existence of which we are a part.

Unitarian Universalist Association
of Congregations
25 Beacon St.
Boston, MA 02108–2800
(617) 742-2100
www.uua.org

Church of the Larger Fellowship
25 Beacon St.
Boston, MA 02108–2800
(617) 948-6166
www.clfuu.org

NOTES

# NOTES

NOTES

We gratefully acknowledge permission to reprint the following materials: Reflections by Rebekah A. Montgomery, Thomas R. Beall, Floyd Vernon Chandler, Laurel Hallman, David Pyle, Barbara Merritt, Jeffrey Alan Lockwood; Xolani Kacela, Cynthia L.G. Kane, Kelly Cummins-Pickens; excerpt from *What God Is Like* by James Dillet Freeman, used with permission of Unity, www.unity.org; "A Prayer for Desert Times" by Margaret Keip; "Prayer for Memorial Day" by Wayne Arnason; "Inevitably our anguish . . ." by Paul Carnes, reprinted by permission of Molly Carnes; "During Wartime" by M. Susan Milnor; prayer by M. Susan Milnor; "Memorial Day Prayer" by Barbara Pescan; prayer by Sydney K. Wilde; 22 lines from "The Way" in *Collected Poems* by Edwin Muir, p. 138, © Faber and Faber, Ltd., reprinted by permission of Oxford University Press, Inc.; "The Avowal" by Denise Levertov, from *The Stream and the Sapphire*, copyright © 1984 by Denise Levertov, reprinted by permission of New Directions Publishing Corp.; "The Young Dead Soldiers" from *Collected Poems, 1917–1982* by Archibald MacLeish, copyright © 1985 by The Estate of Archibald MacLeish, reprinted by permission of Houghton Mifflin Harcourt Publishing Company, all rights reserved; New Revised Standard Version Bible, copyright 1989, Division of Christian Education of the National Council of the Churches of Christ in the United States of America, used by permission, all rights reserved; "The Peace of Wild Things" copyright © 1985 by Wendell Berry, from *The Collected Poems of Wendell Berry, 1957–1982* by Wendell Berry, reprinted by permission of Counterpoint.